Original title:
Wishes on the Night Wind

Copyright © 2024 Creative Arts Management OÜ
All rights reserved.

Author: Alec Donovan
ISBN HARDBACK: 978-9916-90-540-1
ISBN PAPERBACK: 978-9916-90-541-8

The Moon's Gentle Promises

In the stillness of the night,
The moon whispers soft secrets,
Casting silver on the lake,
Dreams awaken in the waters.

With each glow, a promise made,
Guiding hearts through shadows deep,
A beacon for the lost souls,
In twilight's embrace, we trust.

Sylphs of the Evening Sky

Dancing lights in the dark,
Echoes of laughter and grace,
Whispers of soft, warm breezes,
Carried forth through the dusk.

They twirl 'round the stars, aglow,
Singing of freedom and dreams,
Fluttering like petals in spring,
Chasing the night, wild and free.

Echoes of Distant Desires

A heartbeat reaches for the stars,
Longing for places unseen,
Every sigh a silent wish,
Resonating through the years.

Memories painted in twilight,
Stirring deep within the heart,
Each echo a fleeting moment,
Calling us to chase the light.

Over the Tranquil Horizon

Hues of orange brush the sky,
As the sun kisses the day goodbye,
Ripples dance upon the sea,
A gentle farewell to the light.

With the night, a calm descends,
Wrapping earth in a tender hug,
Stars emerge like scattered dreams,
Guiding us to the night's embrace.

Enchanted Night's Reverie

Under the moonlight's soft glow,
Whispers of dreams begin to flow.
Stars twinkle with secrets untold,
In this realm, magic unfolds.

A breeze carries scents of the night,
Guiding our hearts to take flight.
Mirrored dreams on silver streams,
As we wander through starlit beams.

Lost in a world of wonder, calm,
Nature's hymns, a soothing balm.
Wrapped in shadows, we ignite,
This enchanted night's pure delight.

Treasures in the Darkest Hours

When shadows stretch and silence reigns,
Hope ignites amidst the pains.
In the depths, our spirits shine,
Unveiling treasures that are divine.

Each sigh holds a glimmer of grace,
A gentle light in a sacred space.
As darkness dances with despair,
We find the strength that lingers there.

Embrace the night, let worries cease,
Within the chaos lies our peace.
In every tear, every scar,
We discover who we truly are.

Harmony of Wishes Held aloft

In twilight's embrace, wishes soar,
Crafted dreams at destiny's door.
With hearts aligned and spirits bright,
We send our hopes into the night.

Like fireworks across the dark sky,
Whirling colors as they fly.
Each desire, a star in the vast,
A symphony of futures cast.

Together we sing, voices unite,
Our aspirations take their flight.
In the dance of shadows and light,
We find harmony in the night.

The Dance of Dreams Beneath the Stars

Guided by twinkling lights above,
We step into the night with love.
With every twirl and every sway,
Dreams awaken, come what may.

The world spins softly, time slows down,
In this moment, we wear no crown.
With hearts as free as the open air,
We lose ourselves in the night's glare.

Together we weave tales so bright,
In a dance that feels just right.
Beneath the stars, dreams take flight,
As we twine in the silent night.

Melodies of the Quiet Night

In the stillness, soft winds play,
Whispers wrapped in shadows lay.
Moonlight weaves a silver thread,
Crickets sing as day has fled.

Beneath the stars, the world is bright,
Dreams take wing in velvet night.
A symphony of silent sighs,
The heart awakens, love replies.

Secrets Carried by the Stars

In the sky, secrets twinkle clear,
Stories ancient, drawing near.
Galaxies spin in endless dance,
Each twinkle holds a whispered chance.

From distant worlds, they send their light,
Guiding souls through the endless night.
In the gaze of their radiant glow,
Dreamers find the paths to go.

The Silent Call of the Cosmos

The cosmos calls with gentle grace,
In the darkness, we find our place.
Planets hum in quiet tune,
Echoes drift from sun to moon.

As stardust swirls in cosmic flight,
Hope ignites in the starry night.
A universe vast, alive, and free,
Invites our hearts to dream and see.

Hopes that Drift Like Fireflies

In the dusk, fireflies gleam,
Luminous hopes in twilight's dream.
Wings that flicker, soft and light,
Bringing joy to the falling night.

Chasing whispers through the trees,
Each glow a wish upon the breeze.
They dance and spin, a fleeting sight,
Reminding us of pure delight.

Fantasies on the Gentle Gale

Whispers dance upon the breeze,
Carrying dreams from distant seas.
Each rustle speaks of tales untold,
In the twilight, our hopes unfold.

Clouds drift softly through the sky,
Wings of wishes learning to fly.
In every sigh, a heart does soar,
Beneath the stars forevermore.

Shadows of Love in Dusk's Glow

As daylight fades to a gentle hue,
In the dim light, love feels so true.
Soft silhouettes begin to play,
Promises whispering night and day.

Hand in hand, we weave our fate,
In twilight's arms, we patiently wait.
Every glance holds a silent vow,
In shadows deep, we cherish now.

Stars that Listen to Longing Hearts

In the velvet sky, a beacon shines,
A tapestry woven with silver lines.
Each twinkle, a wish we dare to send,
Stars that listen, our faithful friends.

Hearts beat softly, a rhythmic dance,
Under their gaze, we take our chance.
With every pulse, our dreams ignite,
The cosmos answers, holding us tight.

Gentle Night's Embrace

The moon cradles the world in light,
Wrapping all in a soft midnight.
Stars sprinkle joy on sleepy eyes,
As dreams unfold in starlit skies.

A lullaby sings through the trees,
Carried forth by the tender breeze.
In gentle night, the heart finds peace,
Moments linger, and worries cease.

Murmurs of Heart's Contemplation

In quiet whispers, we confide,
The secrets held, the truths inside.
A gentle pulse beneath the night,
Our souls unite, the world alight.

In shadows cast, our fears take flight,
We navigate through dreams so bright.
Each thought a stone, within the stream,
A tapestry of hope and dream.

Floating Thoughts Along the Horizon

With every wave that kisses sand,
The fleeting thoughts slip through my hand.
They voyage far, where skies are wide,
Embracing change, like ebbing tide.

In colors bold, the sunset bleeds,
Each hue, it sows the heart's own seeds.
A tapestry of wishes made,
In twilight's glow, new dreams cascade.

Adrift in the Celestial Symphony

The stars align, a cosmic dance,
Each twinkle holds a tale of chance.
In silence deep, the universe hums,
A melody where quiet comes.

Among the clouds, my spirit soars,
Through galaxies and open doors.
Each note a sigh, a breath of space,
In harmony, I find my place.

Sojourn of Dreams in the Moonlight

Beneath the moon's soft, silver gaze,
We wander through the night's embrace.
With whispered vows, our hopes take flight,
In shadows cast, we chase the light.

Each dream a lantern, glowing bright,
Illuminating the path of night.
In laughter shared and silence known,
Together here, we find our home.

Quiet Echoes of What Could Be

In shadows cast by dreams untold,
A whisper stirs, both brave and bold.
Faint glimmers of what lies ahead,
In silence, hopes and wishes thread.

Time dances softly, moments weave,
In every heart, the urge to believe.
The past a dream, the future clear,
In every echo, possibilities near.

The Softness of Moonlit Sighs

Beneath the stars, a gentle glow,
The world at rest, in tranquil flow.
Moonlit whispers, secrets shared,
In tender moments, souls are bared.

Night wraps the earth in a soft embrace,
Each sigh a note in time and space.
Dreams drift lightly, like silver streams,
In the quiet night, we dance in dreams.

Fables Carried on the Zephyr

Stories ride on winds so light,
Carried forth into the night.
Whispers of the past unfold,
In every tale, a heart of gold.

The zephyr speaks of love and loss,
Of paths we choose and paths we cross.
With every breeze, a truth we find,
In tales of fate, our lives entwined.

Moonbeams and Heartbeats

Under the moon's soft, silken thread,
Heartbeat rhythms, gently spread.
Each pulse a story, every sigh,
In this stillness, dreams can fly.

Embrace the night, let shadows play,
As moonbeams guide our thoughts away.
In fleeting moments, love ignites,
In harmony with the starry nights.

Beneath the Canvas of Night

Stars whisper secrets, soft and bright,
Their glimmers dance in the velvet night.
Moonlight weaves tales on the earth,
A silent witness to the cosmos' birth.

Shadows play games under the sky,
Dreams take flight as the night winds sigh.
Each heartbeat echoes a timeless beat,
In the quiet embrace, our spirits meet.

Stardust Messages to the Cosmos

Scattered across the heavens so wide,
Stardust carries hopes on each cosmic ride.
Wishes arise on the wings of the breeze,
In the infinity, whispers seek to please.

Galaxies swirl in a cosmic ballet,
Transcending boundaries, they gently sway.
Messages linger in the vastness above,
A tapestry woven with dreams and love.

Veils of Enchantment at Dusk

As daylight fades and shadows grow,
Veils of enchantment begin to flow.
Colors bleed softly in the twilight's grace,
Nature unfolds in a tender embrace.

Whispers of magic fill the cool air,
Each sigh of the world a soft, sweet prayer.
Moments linger like dew on a leaf,
In the serenity, we find our belief.

Silent Yearnings in the Stillness

In the quiet moments, hearts conspire,
Silent yearnings spark a soft fire.
Eyes closed gently, dreams take their wing,
In the stillness, we learn to sing.

Time pauses, wrapped in tender night,
Whispers of longing bathe us in light.
Each heartbeat echoes, hope in the dark,
In the silence, we find our spark.

Musing Beneath Heaven's Dome

Under a sky so vast and wide,
Whispers of the stars collide.
Thoughts drifting like clouds above,
In this stillness, I find love.

Moments pause in twilight's grace,
Reflecting dreams I cannot trace.
Each twinkling light, a silent muse,
Guiding me where I must choose.

Gentle breezes softly sigh,
Carrying secrets from the sky.
Here in solitude, I roam,
Always searching for my home.

Beneath the dome where hopes reside,
Navigating with the stars as guide.
In this cosmos, vast and bright,
I weave my dreams through the night.

Night's Whispered Confessions

In shadows deep, the night unfolds,
A tapestry of tales untold.
The moonlight spills its soft embrace,
Whispering secrets in this space.

Stars alight with glowing grace,
Comfort found in their still place.
Every twinkle, a silent plea,
Under the velvet canopy.

Voices dance upon the breeze,
Carried softly through the trees.
Every sigh a truth confessed,
In the night, we find our rest.

From shadows emerge the dreams we seek,
Emboldened whispers, tender and meek.
Through the stillness, hearts take flight,
In the depths of comforting night.

Unfolding Dreams in Starlit Stillness

Glimmers of hope in the quiet air,
Where dreams unfold with utmost care.
Starlit nights weave tales untold,
In the silence, futures unfold.

A blanket of darkness, serene and calm,
Wrapping the world in a soothing balm.
Each breath a wish into the deep,
Where secrets of the cosmos sleep.

Twinkling lights ignite the soul,
In their warmth, we become whole.
Navigating through this cosmic sea,
Finding fragments of destiny.

Here in stillness, hearts ignite,
With fervor born of the soft night.
Unfolding dreams that brightly gleam,
In the vast expanse of the starlit dream.

The Glow of Heartfelt Longings

A glow emerges in the quiet night,
Yearnings whisper, taking flight.
Each flicker speaks of dreams alive,
In the stillness, hopes survive.

Beneath the stars, desires bloom,
Bringing warmth within the gloom.
A symphony of wishes flow,
Illuminating what we know.

Within the heart, a radiant spark,
Guiding through the shadows dark.
Every longing softly flows,
In the glow, true beauty grows.

Here in the stillness, hearts align,
With every ache, a love divine.
In the quiet, we find our way,
Embraced by the glow of yesterday.

Hopes Encased in the Night's Embrace

In the silence of dusk, dreams unfold,
Whispers of wishes in shadows retold.
Moonlight weaves tales of what could be,
Hopes encased in a night's gentle plea.

Stars wink softly, secrets to share,
Carrying visions through cool evening air.
Each heartbeat paired with celestial flight,
Wrapped in the warmth of the night's sweet light.

Stars as Dispatchers of Longing

Twinkling observers watch from above,
Send messages wrapped in starlit love.
Each shimmering point a longing anew,
Echoes of hearts that once brightly flew.

They trace the paths of silent desires,
Kindling within us unquenchable fires.
Drawing our dreams from the depths of the day,
Stars as dispatchers, guiding the way.

Shadows of Desire Beneath Cosmic Canopies

Under vast skies where the cosmos reigns,
Shadows of desire dance in moonlit chains.
Night's gentle touch brings whispers of lust,
As hearts intertwine in passion's soft dust.

Galaxies bloom with the beat of our souls,
Woven together, making us whole.
Each star a witness to secrets we share,
Beneath cosmic canopies, love laid bare.

The Night's Potion of Dreams

In twilight's potion, we drift and we sway,
Caught in the magic of night's gentle play.
Visions arise like clouds in the air,
As the heart revels in dreams laid bare.

With each soft breath, reality fades,
Into the depths where enchantment cascades.
The night sings softly, cerulean balm,
Cradling our spirits, a soothing calm.

Nightfall's Hidden Ambitions

Shadows stretch as daylight fades,
Whispers dance among the trees.
Secrets wrapped in evening's cloak,
Dreams awaken with the breeze.

Stars ignite the velvet sky,
Guiding thoughts that drift and soar.
In the stillness, hopes align,
Fated wishes to explore.

Night unveils its deep allure,
Mysteries drift on velvet wings.
In the silence, hearts secure,
The night holds all that dreaming brings.

Through the dark, ambitions glow,
Illuminating paths unknown.
In the night's embrace, we grow,
Finding strength in dreams we've sown.

Tides of Hope Underneath the Moon

Waves cascade on sandy shores,
Carrying whispers from the deep.
Moonlight dances, gently pours,
Cradling secrets as we sleep.

Tides reveal what hearts can't show,
Embers of dreams on waters gleam.
In the night, we feel the flow,
Guided by each silent beam.

Stars above like scattered seeds,
Planted in the ocean's dance.
Hope is found in gentle creeds,
In moonlit moments, we take chance.

Beneath the sky's vast, endless hue,
We find a world of endless grace.
Tides of hope, both old and new,
Embrace us in a warm embrace.

The Calling of Night's Serenade

In the hush of twilight's breath,
Softly, come the notes of night.
Melodies arise from death,
Whispered tunes, a sweet delight.

Crickets play their timeless song,
Leaves rustle, weaving through the air.
In the dark, we all belong,
To the serenade, we share.

Moonbeams cast a silver veil,
Guiding spirits on their way.
Every note, a gentle trail,
Leading dreams until the day.

Embrace the calling of the night,
Let the music swell inside.
Serenades take flight in flight,
In the dark, our souls abide.

Lull of the Velvety Night

Veils of dusk, a calming shroud,
Softly wraps the world in dreams.
In stillness, whispers sing aloud,
Cradled deep in silent streams.

Stars like diamonds pierce the dark,
Gently lulling hearts to rest.
In night's embrace, we leave a mark,
Finding solace, feeling blessed.

Every sigh a soothing breeze,
Each heartbeat synchronized with time.
In the calm, the mind finds peace,
Wrapped in night's enchanting rhyme.

Lulled by shades of endless night,
Drifting in the arms of grace.
Here we seek the purest light,
As sleep transcends in soft embrace.

Celestial Currents of Heartfelt Hopes

In the night sky, wishes alight,
Stars twinkle softly, dreams take flight.
A gentle breeze whispers through trees,
Hope flows like rivers, endless and free.

Moonbeams dance on silver streams,
Carrying visions, igniting gleams.
Hearts pulse with light, warm and divine,
In this embrace, our spirits entwine.

Galaxies spin in sweet serenades,
Each note a promise, in twilight cascades.
Beyond the vastness, we find our way,
Guided by love, come what may.

With every heartbeat, a story unfolds,
Celestial currents, our fate it beholds.
Together we'll soar, on wings of pure hope,
In the tapestry of time, forever we cope.

Flickers of Light in the Abyss

In shadows deep, where silence dwells,
Flickers of light break haunting spells.
A spark ignites in murky nights,
Guiding lost souls to newfound heights.

Whispers of courage stir the air,
Banish despair with loving care.
Each flicker burns with fierce intent,
Hope rises strong; it's heaven-sent.

A dance of shadows, a ballet bold,
Tales of resilience, silently told.
Through the darkness, we shall persist,
For every flicker is a hopeful tryst.

With each heartbeat, our spirits soar,
Illuminating paths forevermore.
In the abyss, let light collide,
Together, hand in hand, we'll abide.

Melodies of Midnight's Heart

Under a blanket of starlit dreams,
Midnight's heart hums with soft gleams.
Each note a whisper, a gentle sigh,
Playing the rhythm that makes us fly.

In the quiet, melodies unfold,
Stories of love, both tender and bold.
Stars join in, harmonizing the night,
Creating a symphony, pure and bright.

Time stands still in the dusky embrace,
Every beat savored, every trace.
The moon presides, a conductor wise,
Guiding our dreams through velvet skies.

As night deepens, our hearts take wing,
To the sweet serenade that midnight sings.
With melodies woven, we drift apart,
Carried forever by midnight's heart.

Whirlwinds of Hope Across the Sky

Whirlwinds gather, swirling with chance,
Carrying whispers of a hopeful dance.
In tempest's embrace, we find our way,
With courage rising to greet the day.

Clouds paint stories, of dreams unspun,
Chasing the horizon, we greet the sun.
Each gust a promise, a daring flight,
Propelling us forward into the light.

Through storms we travel, hearts strong and true,
In the chaos, love finds its view.
With every turn, the winds bestow,
A tapestry woven with seeds we sow.

Across the sky, our spirits glide,
In whirlwinds of hope, we boldly ride.
Together we'll soar, embracing the sky,
For in the journey, we learn to fly.

Light Beneath the Restive Clouds

Whispers of dawn break the night,
As shadows retreat, taking flight.
Colors entwine in a soft embrace,
The sky ignites with a radiant face.

Horizon lines pulse with a beat,
Where dreams and reality gently meet.
Each ray of sun a promise unfurled,
A glow that awakens the hidden world.

Storms may gather, fierce and wild,
Yet hope remains, forever a child.
Through tempests and trials, light will prevail,
Beneath the restive, unfolding veil.

In the quiet moments, peace will reign,
As nature breathes, releasing the strain.
With every dawn, a new tale begins,
Light beneath clouds, where joy always wins.

Fancies Set Afloat in the Starry Sea

In the darkness, dreams take flight,
Sailing softly through the night.
Whispers of wishes drift and swirl,
Creating magic in the cosmic pearl.

Stars like lanterns, shining bold,
Each one a story yet untold.
Permissions granted to leap and play,
Fancies afloat in a celestial ballet.

Under the moon's gentle gaze,
Hearts entwined in a lovers' maze.
Galaxies twinkle in sweet refrain,
In the vast expanse where dreams remain.

As tides of time ebb and flow,
Grasp the wonders that softly glow.
In the starry sea, forever we'll drift,
Embracing the night, a luminous gift.

Secrets that Dance in the Gloom

In shadows deep, secrets breathe,
Glimmers of truth, hard to perceive.
Whispers echo in the velvet night,
Dancing softly, just out of sight.

Figures sway in the silence profound,
Mysteries cloaked in whispers found.
A tapestry woven with threads of fate,
Each secret holds a timeless weight.

Through the haze of uncertainty's call,
Voices beckon, enchanting us all.
Beneath the surface, stories entwine,
Secrets that linger, both yours and mine.

As shadows converge, truths shall ignite,
Revealing the beauty hidden from sight.
In the gloom where the heartbeats hum,
Dance with the secrets that quietly come.

Beyond the Shimmering Veil

A curtain of night drapes the land,
Mysteries wait with a gentle hand.
Each shimmer a promise, a truth to unveil,
Whispered softly, beyond the veil.

Glances exchanged in a fleeting glance,
Where echoes of fate lead the dance.
Stars and shadows play their role,
In the depths of darkness, the heart finds its soul.

The shimmer of light, a beacon so bright,
Guides us through the enveloping night.
With every step toward the unknown,
We find the strength to be fully grown.

Beyond the veil lies a world reborn,
With hopes anew in the light of dawn.
As dreams awaken and fears start to fade,
In the shimmer of life, we are unafraid.

Flickers of Fancy in the Dark

In the hush of midnight skies,
Whispers dance and gently sigh,
Thoughts like fireflies take flight,
Flickers bright in soft twilight.

Shadows stretch and shadows play,
Crafting dreams that drift away,
Chasing echoes in the night,
Fleeting visions, pure delight.

Stars ignite the velvet shroud,
Casting hopes that feel so proud,
In this realm where wishes gleam,
Silent pulses spark the dream.

As the world holds its breath tight,
Imagination blooms in flight,
Flickers melt into the dawn,
Bringing forth a brand new song.

Breath of the Night's Embrace

Moonlight weaves a silken thread,
Caressing dreams in softest bed,
Every heartbeat, sweet and slow,
A lullaby that starts to flow.

Silence drapes the world in peace,
Moments linger, time's release,
Whispers gilded, soft and low,
Breath of night begins to glow.

Among the stars a story told,
Of lovers' hearts and dreams of old,
Wrapped in midnight's sweet caress,
Every breath a soft confess.

In this haven, fears deflate,
Love ignites and merges fate,
Night's embrace, where dreams arise,
In the stillness, we collide.

Dreams Adrift in the Cosmic Sea

Waves of stardust, soft and bright,
Carry thoughts through endless night,
Navigating through the skies,
Where the boundless dreamer lies.

Galaxies spin, a cosmic dance,
Every star a hidden chance,
Floating dreams like ships at sea,
Lost in tranquil mystery.

Nebulas cradle hopes anew,
Each aspiration, deep and true,
In the void, the whispers twine,
Painting visions, bold and fine.

Sailing on this starry tide,
In the silence, we'll confide,
Dreams adrift, eternally,
In the heart of mystery.

Secrets Untold Beneath the Stars

Beneath the veil of twilight's grace,
Hidden truths find their place,
In the shadows, stories weave,
Tales of hearts that dare believe.

Constellations hold the key,
To the secrets wild and free,
Echoes from the depths of time,
Resonating in whispers' rhyme.

Galaxies in silence speak,
Of the dreams that we all seek,
In every twinkle, stories dwell,
Secrets wrapped in starlit spell.

Held in night's enchanting thrall,
Underneath, we hear the call,
Secrets shared beneath the stars,
Binding fate, despite the scars.

The Lullaby of Unsung Prayers

In the hush of night, whispers dwell,
Silent hopes cast under a spell.
Each gentle sigh a wish takes flight,
Nurtured dreams dance in the light.

Cradled softly in twilight's embrace,
Voices of longing fill empty space.
Beneath the stars, hearts beat in tune,
Resonant echoes beneath the moon.

Tears blend with laughter, joy and despair,
Each moment woven with tender care.
In shadows deep, where secrets lay,
Unsung prayers find their way.

Awakened by the dawn's soft kiss,
Fleeting thoughts of forgotten bliss.
With every sunrise, hopes renew,
The lullaby sings, forever true.

Wishes Cast Upon the Gales

Upon the winds, I send my plea,
A whisper carried across the sea.
Dreams take flight on a gentle breeze,
Fleeting moments, like rustling leaves.

Stars above with eyes so bright,
Catch my wishes, guiding light.
In this dance of fate and chance,
Each desire sways in a timeless trance.

Mountains echo, valleys reply,
As I seek a world where the heart can fly.
With every gust that bends the trees,
Hope is woven in the fabric of these.

Let the surf's roar be my guide,
In waves of ambition, I will not hide.
Casting wishes where the gales unfold,
Stories of dreams forever told.

Celestial Secrets in the Breeze

Whispers linger in the twilight air,
Secrets of cosmos, shimmering rare.
Stars converse in a quiet glow,
Ancient tales of the heavens flow.

Each breeze carries a starry tale,
Of love and loss, where dreams prevail.
Listen closely as night unveils,
Mysteries woven in shimmering trails.

The moonlight drapes a silver veil,
Over wonders hidden, soft and frail.
Celestial rhythm, a sacred dance,
In the breeze, find the heart's true chance.

Beneath the sky, with hope anew,
We gather the scents of midnight dew.
In silence, the universe does tease,
With celestial secrets in the breeze.

Ethereal Cries Beneath the Stars

In the velvet night, shadows creep,
Hearts awake while the world sleeps.
Ethereal cries, soft and low,
Echo through valleys where moonlight flows.

Stars twinkle with stories untold,
Guiding lost souls, brave and bold.
Each whisper a spark in the dark,
Filling the silence, igniting a spark.

Winds carry laughter, sorrow, and dreams,
Like elusive prisms with endless beams.
Under the canopy of the night,
Lives intertwine in a dance of light.

Beneath the heavens, we stand and pray,
For solace, for peace to show the way.
Ethereal cries weave through the night,
In this vast cosmos, we find our light.

Songs of Untold Dreams at Dusk

In twilight's glow, shadows play,
A whispering breeze sweeps the day.
Hidden hopes in the fading light,
Dancing softly, hearts take flight.

Colors merge, the sky's canvas bleeds,
A chorus of thoughts, unspoken needs.
With every sigh, a story begins,
As day departs, the night softly spins.

Stars awaken, their secrets unfold,
In dreams, our stories are quietly told.
Echoes of laughter, glimmers of grace,
In dusk's embrace, we find our place.

So let us sing, through shadows and light,
Of untold dreams that dance in the night.
Together we wander, hand in hand,
In the realm where wishes take a stand.

The Tides of Night's Embrace

Moonbeams shimmer on rippling seas,
Whispers linger on the cool night breeze.
The tides of time, they ebb and flow,
Carrying dreams where wanderers go.

Softly the waves kiss the shore,
A lullaby sweet, forevermore.
In depths of silence, secrets are stirred,
In the heart of darkness, our voices heard.

Night's embrace, a tender hold,
Stories of lovers, timeless and bold.
Ephemeral moments, fleeting yet near,
In the ocean of stars, we shed the fear.

With every tide, our souls are free,
Boundless like the deep blue sea.
Together we drift on this endless dream,
In night's embrace, love's eternal theme.

Whispers of Celestial Dreams

In the hush of night, dreams take flight,
Whispers of stars glow with delight.
Each twinkle carries a wish profound,
In cosmic silence, our hearts resound.

Galaxies spin in their timeless dance,
Invisible threads pull us to chance.
In the vastness, we find our truth,
A tapestry woven from our youth.

Beyond the clouds, where hopes converge,
Celestial visions begin to surge.
With every heartbeat, the universe sways,
In dreams, we seek the light of new days.

So let us wander in this celestial stream,
Chasing the echoes of our dreams.
In the infinite night, we rise and gleam,
Finding our place in the starlit beam.

Secrets Carried by Starlight

Silent whispers weave through the air,
Secrets ignited, moments laid bare.
Starlight dances on the velvet sky,
Carrying tales that never die.

Each sparkling flicker, a glimpse of fate,
In midnight's glow, our souls await.
Hushed confessions in the midnight hour,
Beneath the stars, we find our power.

In cosmic shadows, the past entwined,
Memories linger, forever aligned.
With every twinkle, a new path glows,
A map of dreams that softly flows.

So here we stand, where starlight spills,
Embraced by the night, our heartbeats thrill.
In whispered secrets, love understands,
We're carried by starlight, hand in hand.

Cradle of the Midnight Moon

In the stillness of the night,
The moon cradles dreams,
Whispers soft as feathered light,
Glimmers of ancient themes.

Stars above begin to hum,
A lullaby so sweet,
Crickets join, their voices drum,
Nature's heart skips a beat.

Shadowed trees dance in sway,
Underneath that silver glow,
Night embraces the weary day,
In a world only moonbeams know.

With every flicker, every spark,
Hope ignites in silent flight,
Cradle me until it's dark,
Hold me close, dear midnight light.

Lament of the Shooting Stars

Across the canvas, tears of light,
Fleeting wishes take their wing,
In moments brief, then into night,
A chorus lost, yet hearts do sing.

Echoes of dreams that drift away,
Whispers carried on the breeze,
Each star a story, gone astray,
Lamenting softly through the trees.

Eyes raised high in silent prayer,
For wishes cast on glowing trails,
A glimpse of hope in velvet air,
Where time forgets, and silence prevails.

In the darkness, skin to skin,
The cosmos breathes in twilight's glow,
For every end, a new begin,
As shooting stars weave tales below.

Glimmers Wrapped in Darkness

Amidst the shadows, secrets hide,
Glimmers twinkling, softly found,
In whispers where the night abides,
    Lives the magic, profound.

Veils of mist around us cling,
A shroud of dreams, so bittersweet,
Yet in silence, spirits sing,
As darkness dances at our feet.

Stars will flicker, hearts will pause,
Cloaked in wonder, veiled in grace,
Every sigh, a cosmic cause,
A gentle nudge through time and space.

In this realm of hope and dread,
The night conceals what day reveals,
Glimmers bought from dreams once shed,
Wrapped in darkness, the heart heals.

Serenade of an Unseen Breeze

Beyond the trees, a whisper flows,
A serenade, soft and low,
Dancing leaves in gentle prose,
The world feels light, the worries slow.

Each note a sigh, a lover's dream,
Carrying tales through twilight haze,
An unseen force, a velvet stream,
Rustling secrets in soft praise.

In the quiet, shadows sway,
Guided by an unseen hand,
Nature's voice will lead the way,
Across the vast, embracing land.

Listen close, the heart will hear,
The breeze that dances in the dark,
An anthem sweet, a song sincere,
The unseen breeze ignites the spark.

Gentle Serenade of the Night

The moonlight softly weaves,
A tapestry of dreams rare,
Whispers ride the evening breeze,
Heartbeats echo in the air.

Stars awaken, one by one,
Painting skies with silver light,
In the stillness, hopes are spun,
Serenading the velvet night.

Crickets play their sweet refrain,
Nature's chorus, pure delight,
Each note dances with no chain,
Boundless in this tranquil flight.

In the dark, a promise glows,
Of tomorrows yet unseen,
In this gentle hug, it grows,
Holding dreams like it's a dream.

Timeless Hopes on Gentle Zephyrs

Softly blow the zephyrs free,
Carrying whispers of the dawn,
Promises that always be,
Binding hearts where dreams are drawn.

Clouds float by, like fleeting thoughts,
A canvas for the sun's embrace,
In the dance, the soul is caught,
Time surrenders, finding grace.

Beneath the boughs, a secret shared,
With every breeze, a tale unfolds,
Hope ignites, forever dared,
In the warmth, a spark of gold.

Endless skies above our heads,
Kissing dreams with each caress,
In the silence, nothing dreads,
Timeless hopes will find their rest.

Flickering Lanterns of Longing

In the dark, lanterns sway,
Flickering like hearts in pain,
Each glow tells a story, they say,
Of love lost in the rain.

Shadows dance with whispered sighs,
Drawing lines between the near,
In the stillness, silence lies,
Holding dreams that disappear.

Through the night, a journey calls,
Pathways glimmer in the mist,
Guiding souls where memory falls,
In the tender, soft twilight kissed.

Hope remains, though fleeting light,
Now a beacon in the gloom,
Flickering lanterns, pure and bright,
Guide us gently through the room.

Midnight's Breath of Aspiration

As midnight approaches, still and deep,
A breath of dreams begins to rise,
In the silence, secrets keep,
Aspiring whispers paint the skies.

The stars align like thoughts unfurl,
Casting wishes in the night,
Every spark a precious pearl,
Igniting futures, burning bright.

Moonbeams drape the world in peace,
Cradling hopes in soft embrace,
In this moment, troubles cease,
Time stands still in a sacred space.

With every heartbeat, courage grows,
Midnight's breath, a gentle guide,
For in the dark, ambition flows,
Setting dreams on paths so wide.

Petals in the Velvet Breeze

In the garden where flowers sway,
Soft whispers dance in light of day.
Petals flutter, colors bloom,
Nature's cradle, sweet perfume.

Beneath the arch of azure skies,
Gentle breezes hold the cries.
Rustling leaves tell tales of old,
Secrets of the heart unfold.

As twilight softens every hue,
Stars emerge, the night anew.
Silhouettes of dreams take flight,
In the calm of fading light.

With every gust that brushes near,
Memories linger, soft and clear.
Embracing moments, fleeting still,
Time's gentle touch, a tender thrill.

Moonlit Aspirations

Upon the lake, the silver glows,
Illuminating where hope flows.
Dreams arise on the shimmering tide,
With the moon, our thoughts confide.

Whispers travel on the night air,
Carrying wishes beyond compare.
Stars twinkle with a knowing gaze,
Guiding hearts through shadowed maze.

In the hush of midnight's breath,
Every silence hints at depth.
Visions painted bright and bold,
Unfold like stories yet untold.

With hearts aligned, we chase the light,
Wandering souls in the velvet night.
Embracing dreams, we dare to soar,
Fingers reaching evermore.

Serenade of the Midnight Air

Under the moon's silvery kiss,
Nighttime sighs, a timeless bliss.
Crickets sing in soft embrace,
Nature's hymn in a sacred space.

Stars like diamonds, bold and clear,
Whisper secrets to those who hear.
Every note a gentle kiss,
In this night, we find our bliss.

Shadows dance on leaves above,
Wrapped in twilight's tender love.
Harmony flows through every vein,
In this serenade, we remain.

As the world begins to rest,
Silent dreams reveal their quest.
Captured moments in the dark,
Igniting souls with every spark.

Flickering Hopes in Twilight

As the sun dips low, shadows play,
Fingers trace the dusk's ballet.
Glimmers of hope break through the cloud,
In whispered thoughts, we feel so proud.

Candles flicker, shadows blend,
In the glow, our dreams extend.
Each flame a wish, each spark a prayer,
Carried softly on the evening air.

Golden hues fade into night,
Yet stars above ignite our sight.
Wandering souls, we chase the glow,
Finding warmth in paths we sow.

With every heartbeat, we ignite,
Flickering hopes in the still of the night.
Together we stand, hand in hand,
Bound by dreams that never strand.

Secrets Carried by Starlight

Beneath the vast and velvet sky,
Whispers drift on wings of night.
Stars conceal what hearts hold dear,
Secrets bloom in silence here.

In shadows cast by silver beams,
Mysteries float like distant dreams.
Eyes that speak without a sound,
In twilight's arms, the truth is found.

Each twinkle tells a story bright,
Of love and loss and fragile light.
Underneath this infinite dome,
Warm secrets guide us safely home.

Whispers Through Moonlit Breezes

In the cool embrace of night,
Moans of wind, a sweet delight.
Leaves that dance with gentle sighs,
Tell the tales of love that flies.

Moonlit paths where shadows play,
Guide our steps till break of day.
Whispers linger in the air,
Hearts entwined without a care.

Echoes soft of voices past,
In this moment, time holds fast.
Underneath the celestial glow,
Secrets shared, forever flow.

Dreams Brewed in Twilight Shadows

As day gives way to night's embrace,
Dreams begin their gentle chase.
In the twilight's softest hue,
Magic stirs, awakening too.

Hushed are hopes that softly gleam,
In the shadows, whispering themes.
Each thought a brew of wonder's spark,
Carried forth into the dark.

Time stands still in this enchanted space,
Reality fades, finds its place.
Through the veil, the visions weave,
Holding dreams, we dare believe.

Echoes of Desire in the Dark

In the stillness where shadows loom,
Yearning hearts are set to bloom.
Each pulse a beat, a whispered call,
Desire's echo enchants us all.

Fingers brush 'neath cover night,
Promises born in moonbeam light.
Every sigh a longing song,
In this moment, we belong.

But shadows flicker, time runs thin,
Yet the fire continues within.
In this dance of fleeting spark,
We find our truth within the dark.

Dreamcatcher of the Night Sky

In shadows deep, the dreams take flight,
A woven web, catching the light.
Stars whisper softly, secrets untold,
Night's gentle embrace, a tale to unfold.

Through silver threads, the wishes glide,
In the quiet dark, where hopes abide.
Each fluttering dream, a spark in the air,
Held close in the heart, wrapped with care.

Ethereal visions dance on the breeze,
Carried on whispers of rustling trees.
Like stardust sprinkled on silken strands,
Dreamcatcher guiding with tender hands.

So let the night wrap you up tight,
In the warmth of dreams, take your flight.
Embrace the magic that midnight brings,
As a dreamcatcher weaves on angel's wings.

Twilight's Promise Wrapped in Silk

Twilight descends, a tender embrace,
Colors that shimmer, a soft, warm grace.
The horizon blushes, painting the view,
Whispers of hope in the evening dew.

Wrapped in silk, the night begins,
A canvas of dreams where magic spins.
The stars emerge, in velvet skies,
Each one a promise, where wonder lies.

Moonbeams dance on the tranquil lake,
Silhouette shadows, the night to awake.
In whispered breezes, a melody sweet,
Nature's own lullaby, soft and complete.

Embrace the twilight, the world in sighs,
To find hidden treasures in soft goodbyes.
As day melts away, dreams take their hold,
In twilight's promise, life gently unfolds.

Notes from a Starlit Heart

A melody whispers from realms above,
Composed in twilight, a song of love.
With notes like petals, soft and light,
Starlit heart's longing ignites the night.

In every heartbeat, a symphony plays,
Echoing softly through countless ways.
The galaxies hum in shimmering tones,
Creating a tapestry of silent moans.

Reflections of magic in every tear,
Notes from the heavens that time holds dear.
Catch them with kindness, let them reside,
In the depths of spirit, where dreams cannot hide.

Under the sky, where wishes collide,
A starlit heart grows, cannot divide.
Every embrace a note, each kiss a song,
In the symphony of life, we all belong.

A Breath of Secret Hopes

In the quiet moments, hopes take flight,
Carried on breaths into the night.
Whispers of wishes, softly they rise,
Dancing like shadows beneath the skies.

A journey of dreams, where hearts unfold,
Secret desires, both timid and bold.
They weave like threads, a tapestry bright,
In the fabric of dusk, stitched with light.

Each sigh a promise, each gasp a prayer,
Floating on breezes that linger in air.
Gather them gently, treasure them deep,
In the vault of your heart, where they softly sleep.

So take a deep breath, let the secrets soar,
Embrace the unknown, uncover what's more.
For every heartbeat carries a dream,
A breath of secret hopes, like a stream.

Lullabies of the Celestial Dance

In twilight's embrace, stars softly gleam,
Whispering secrets as they rise and dream.
Moonlight cascades in gentle streams,
Guiding lost souls through silver beams.

Waves of starlight lull hearts to rest,
Cradled in silence, the cosmos' quest.
Each twinkle a promise, each shimmer a sigh,
In this vast expanse, we drift and fly.

Nebulae swirl in a cosmic tune,
Dancing with shadows, like night and moon.
With every heartbeat, the galaxies sway,
A lullaby woven where night meets day.

Embrace the stillness, let worries cease,
In the celestial dance, we find our peace.
For in the heavens, love's light will enhance,
Every moment, a part of this dance.

Ethereal Longings on the Breeze

Whispers of longing upon the breeze,
Carrying dreams like autumn leaves.
Through fields of azure, they soar and glide,
A gentle yearning that cannot hide.

Echoes of laughter in the air,
Promises woven without a care.
The scent of blossoms fills the night,
Igniting spirits with pure delight.

Winds of time sweep the shadows away,
Cradling wishes that longed to stay.
As stars twinkle bright in the vast sky,
Our hearts are lifted, ready to fly.

In each soft murmur, our hopes entwine,
In nature's embrace, the worlds align.
Ethereal whispers in twilight's grace,
Remind us of love's sweet embrace.

Starlit Yearnings

In the hush of night, desires spark,
Glimmers of hope in the depths of dark.
Each star a wish, a tale untold,
A universe wrapped in mysteries bold.

Through velvet skies, our dreams take flight,
Journeying far like birds in the night.
With every heartbeat, our spirits climb,
Tracing the path of the endless time.

Falling stars whisper, "Make a change,"
In the silent moments, the mind can range.
As constellations dance, we find our way,
In starlit yearnings that brightly sway.

A canvas of wishes painted so wide,
Guiding us gently, a celestial tide.
In every flicker, a story ignites,
Starlit yearnings inviting our flights.

Echoes from a Distant Star

Beneath the canopy of cosmic dreams,
Echoes of light shimmer in streams.
Messages carried through the vast unknown,
A connection forged, though worlds are alone.

Whirling galaxies hum a soft tune,
Illuminating paths under the moon.
From depths of night, a call we hear,
Distant whispers that draw us near.

In infinite space, time bends and sways,
Shaping the memories of countless days.
Each pulse of starlight, a tale to tell,
Echoes that resonate, casting a spell.

So let us listen to the silence vast,
Embrace the wonders of the future and past.
For in the shadows of the midnight hour,
Echoes from a star awaken our power.

Midnight's Lantern Burning Bright

A flicker in the darkened sky,
The lantern glows, a soft reply.
It dances with the starlit breeze,
Illuminating shadows with ease.

Whispers of dreams begin to weave,
In silence, hearts begin to cleave.
A world awake, yet still and deep,
As secrets come, the darkness keeps.

Through wandering paths, the light does guide,
It holds the night, a faithful stride.
Each fluttered ray, a gentle kiss,
In midnight's charm, we find our bliss.

Amid the hush where hopes unite,
We chase the warmth of lantern's light.
In every glow, a tale unfolds,
As midnight's magic softly holds.

Chasing the Quiet Glow of Night

In twilight's hush, the stars align,
We chase the whispers, soft and fine.
The quiet glow enchants our roam,
In distant dreams, we find our home.

The velvet sky, a canvas bright,
With glimmers caught in silver light.
Each breath a pause, a moment sweet,
We flow like rivers, calm and fleet.

Through tangled woods and shadowed lanes,
We chase the glow where magic reigns.
With every step, the night unfolds,
As mysteries and wonders mold.

Together in this serene embrace,
We dance with stars, the night our space.
In quietude, our spirits soar,
Chasing the glow, forevermore.

Whispers in the Enchanted Dark

In the stillness, secrets flow,
Soft whispers in the dark below.
Mysteries wrap like gentle shrouds,
In the silence, our hearts are vowed.

The moonlight spills, a silver thread,
Guiding us where spirits tread.
In shadows' embrace, we find our song,
In enchanted dark, we feel we belong.

Through forest paths and winding trails,
The nightingale's song softly hails.
With every note, the world awakens,
In whispered magic, new dreams are taken.

So let us linger, hand in hand,
In this quiet, enchanted land.
For in the dark, we find our way,
With whispers echoing till the day.

Springing from Shadows of the Moon

From shadows deep, the night unfolds,
A tapestry of stories told.
The moonlight dances on the ground,
Where dreams and wishes can be found.

Springing forth like flowers in bloom,
Across the landscape, dispelling gloom.
Each gentle whisper, a fragile sound,
In lunar glow, our hopes abound.

The night awakens, filled with grace,
While silver beams caress our face.
In this embrace, we take our flight,
Springing from shadows into light.

Beyond the veil, our spirits rise,
With every glance at starlit skies.
As shadows fade, the dawn draws near,
We spring from darkness, free from fear.

The Secrets We Set Adrift

In whispers soft, the secrets lie,
Beneath the waves, where shadows sigh.
A boat of dreams, we gently row,
Setting forth, where wild winds blow.

Each tale we share, a memory spun,
In the twilight, the night begun.
Hearts adrift on shimmering seas,
Finding peace in silent pleas.

With every star, a story told,
Of hidden paths and treasures old.
The tides will guide our drifting fate,
As we embrace the choice we make.

Under the moon, in silver light,
We find our way through endless night.
The secrets kept, now slip away,
Adrift we sail, come what may.

Echoing Lullabies in the Night

The moonlight glows, a soft embrace,
Guiding dreams to a sacred space.
Whispers float on gentle air,
Carried away without a care.

Childhood echoes, pure and sweet,
Dancing softly on silken feet.
Hushed lullabies in shadows play,
Cradled heartbeats drift away.

In the calm of a starry dome,
We find refuge, a fleeting home.
Each note that rings, a tender plea,
Holding tight to what shall be.

As night unfolds its velvet shroud,
We fade away from the restless crowd.
In dreams we sail on silver streams,
Awake to find the heart still gleams.

Harmony of Wishes Floating Free

In twilight's glow, our wishes blend,
Like colors swirling, they transcend.
A dance of hopes on zephyrs ride,
Together casting fears aside.

Every heart, a melody rare,
Echoing softly in the air.
With every beat, a dream ignites,
Painting the world in vibrant lights.

We gather wishes, let them soar,
Like lanterns bright, forevermore.
Against the night, we stand as one,
A symphony until we're done.

The stars above hum sweetly low,
Guiding our dreams as we let go.
In harmony, we'll find our way,
Floating free where night meets day.

Nightfall's Gentle Hues

As dusk descends, the colors blend,
A canvas rich, where shadows mend.
The sky adorned in deep indigo,
Whispers of night in gentle flow.

Soft twilight wraps the world in grace,
Caressing every hidden place.
The stars awake, a twinkling crew,
Embracing all in nightfall's hues.

The cool air sings a soothing tune,
Beneath the watchful eye of the moon.
In every shadow, secrets bloom,
We find our peace in nature's room.

So let us wander, hand in hand,
Through painted skies, a dreamland strand.
With every step, our souls align,
Embracing night, as we entwine.

Milton Keynes UK
Ingram Content Group UK Ltd.
UKHW021927011224
451790UK00005B/55